LOCAL HABITATS

THE
LIVING
RIVER

Nigel Hester

W
FRANKLIN WATTS
LONDON•SYDNEY

This edition 2004

Franklin Watts
96 Leonard Street
London EC2A 4XD

Franklin Watts Australia
45-51 Huntley Street
Alexandria
NSW 2015

Copyright © 1991

First published as Nature Watch: The Living River
Editor: Su Swallow
Designer: K and Co
Illustrations: Angela Owen, Ron Haywood
Phototypeset by Lineage Ltd, Watford

Photography:
Heather Angel 9bl, 10, 11t, 12bl, 13t, 14t, 15tl, 15tr, 20br, 22br, 23t,
27cr, 27b; Ardea 22t, 26br, 28tr, 29c; Bruce Coleman Ltd 12br;
Nigel Hester 4(all), 5(all), 7(both), 8(all), 9t, 9br, 10(inset), 11b, 20t,
20bl, 21, 24t, 24bl, 25tl, 25tr, 25b, 26bl, 27tl, 27tr, 28bl; Eric and
David Hosking/DP Wilson 28br; Frank Lane Picture Agency 16bl, 18br,
21 (inset), 22bl, 23bl, 23br, 28; Robert Pickett 24br; Planet Earth Pictures
21t; Survival Anglia 12t, 13b, 16t, 17 (inset), 18bl, 25tc, 29t.

Front Cover: Heather Angel, Eric and David Hosking (inset right),
Frank Lane Picture Agency (inset left).

A CIP catalogue record for this book is available from the British Library

ISBN: 0 7496 5656 5

Printed in Belgium

CONTENTS

Do you live near a river? Perhaps a river runs through your town or near your village. Have you ever looked closely at your river? What do you know about the plants and animals that live in the water and along the river bank? This book tells you about some of the wildlife to look out for when you are by a river.

Some rivers are not much bigger than a stream, while others are broad stretches of water. The water is fresh, not salty, so some of the plants and animals in rivers are the same as in ponds and lakes. But the water is moving, not still, which creates problems for some wildlife.

The water in this upland river *(top right)* flows quickly downhill. Animals have to cling on tightly to stop themselves being washed away. This lowland river *(below)* flows quite gently. Fish live in the water. Plants grow along the edge and attract insects. Streams *(right)* usually join up to form rivers, and support a rich variety of wildlife.

Fish that are strong swimmers can live in fast-flowing rivers, but smaller creatures may be swept down the river by a fast current. Some live under rocks, or cling to their surface in order to survive. Others can only live safely in slow-moving water. Few plants grow in rushing water, but where the current is slower, plants take root at the water's edge and flourish.

Fast-flowing water does have one advantage for wildlife. As the water splashes over the rocks and pebbles, it traps bubbles of air. This gives the water a high level of oxygen, which all plants and animals need.

Some factories (above) need large amounts of water so they are built beside rivers. If they pump waste materials into the river the water is polluted and plants and animals may die.

Ships (below) can sail up wide, deep rivers to unload at inland ports. Rivers – even quite small ones – are also used for leisure activities such as fishing (left) and boating.

FROM SOURCE TO SEA

Most rivers begin on high ground. Small trickles of water combine to form a stream. The water is shallow and flows quite quickly. Most plants that live here are compact and able to survive if the stream dries up for a short time. Mosses are common in upland streams. Tiny creatures live amongst the moss.

A number of upland streams meet to form a single, fast-flowing river. As the water flows over rocks and stones it carries away any loose soil. It also wears away the rock. When the river eventually reaches flatter ground, the current is slower but the oxygen level is still quite high. Snails, freshwater shrimps and many other animals live in this middle course, feeding on dead plant material washed down by the current. Because the water moves more slowly, some of the silt (fine mud) sinks to the bottom and provides a foothold for some plants.

As the river widens and deepens, the flow of the water slows even more. A lot of silt is deposited and many plants flourish. In some places, the river is very still. Here you can find plants and insects that are common in ponds. The rich supply of food in the lower course attracts many fish.

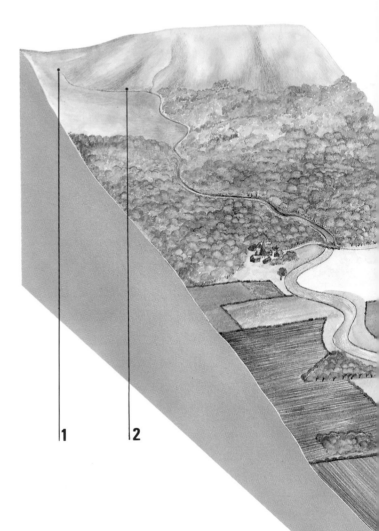

The start point of a river is called the source (1). As the river drops downhill it changes shape and character. It can be divided into three stages. The first stage is the upper course (2). At this point the river is narrow and fairly straight. Then it widens into the middle course (3). As it meanders through the lower course (4), soil is worn away from the outside curve of the bends (5) and deposited on the inside curves (6). Finally, the river flows into the sea at the river mouth (7).

◁ Waterfalls are a very attractive feature of upland rivers. They form where the rock is very hard and does not wear away easily. The splashing water keeps the air moist. This allows mosses and ferns to grow on nearby rocks.

▷ The lower course of a river flows across very flat land. The river meanders (bends) to and fro, taking the easiest route towards the sea.

3

4

5

6

7

The variety of plant life found beside a river depends on two things: the type of soil and the speed of the water flow. Where the river bank is sandy or full of gravel the water quickly wears away the bank. This makes it difficult for plants to take root and grow. In rivers where boating is popular, the wash from fast boats also wears away the river bank, taking any vegetation with it.

Heavy rain can cause the river to swell and wash away bankside vegetation. This often happens in upland areas where rainfall is high and the water level in the river varies. Plants are also lost when cattle trample on them as they drink from the river.

Liverworts *(above)* are simple plants that have no flowers. They often cover rocks by upland streams.

Willow moss *(left)* forms dense bunches up to 1m long in slow-flowing streams and rivers.

▽ Watercress is found in small streams, especially in chalk areas. It can be farmed in special beds *(left)* as a salad crop.

The willow

There are more than 130 species of willow in the world. The weeping willow *(left)*, crack willow and white willow are common by water.

20-spot leaf beetle

sawfly

Many insects rely on willow leaves for their food.

Slow-flowing rivers deposit silt along their length. Plants can take root easily in the silt, especially where the flow is at its slowest. If the flow is very slow, then pond plants become established. Reedbeds can form, providing a home for many nesting birds. Yellow iris and water lily may flower in the summer.

The growth of plants slows the water flow even more, allowing extra silt to build up. In time, a swampy area forms in which trees such as alder and willow can grow.

◁ Purple loosestrife often grows in large clumps beside slow streams and rivers. In summer, its flowers attract many insects, such as the common blue butterfly *(below).*

SURVIVING THE CURRENT

Most river plants produce upright flowers. They rely on the wind or insects to spread pollen from one flower to another so that seeds can form. But most seeds fail to gain a foothold in the moving water and are wasted. So some plants also have another way to reproduce themselves. Small parts of the parent plant break away and root themselves to form new plants. Large clumps of single plants often end up growing together, filling large areas of the river bed.

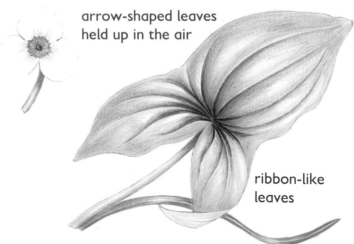

arrow-shaped leaves held up in the air

ribbon-like leaves

△ In slow rivers the arrowhead has two types of leaf. In fast water it only has ribbon-like leaves under water.

▽ There are many types of water crowfoot. River plants can grow to 2m wide and 5m long.

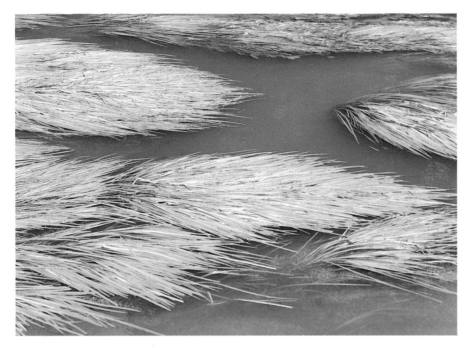

▽ In still or very slow-moving water the unbranched bur-reed grows upright leaves. In fast-flowing water the leaves are long and floating *(left)*, trailing with the current.

Measuring the current

Ask a friend to help you measure the current in a fast-flowing river. Place two canes or sticks 10m apart in the ground along the river bank. Stand by the upstream cane, and drop a twig or leaf into the water. Your friend should stand downstream and use a watch with a second hand to time how long it takes for the twig or leaf to pass the second cane.

If a twig floats 10m in 40 seconds, in one second it will travel 10/40 = ¼m. So in one minute it will travel ¼ x 60 = 15m.

River facts

 The longest river in the world is the Nile, which is 2598km long.

 The highest waterfall in the world is The Angel Falls in Venezuela. Water drops freely for 979m.

 Rivers and streams only account for 0.0001 per cent of all the water in the world.

 The Grand Canyon was formed by the Colorado River, which wore away the rock for 10 million years.

 Nearly three-quarters of the world's fresh water is locked up in glaciers. These are really frozen rivers, and they move a few centimetres every day.

All river creatures face the problem of being washed away by the current. Insects, in particular, are easily carried along by the current because they are small. Few could survive the tumbling water of the upper course of a river, but there is less danger in the middle and lower courses. Even so, they have had to adapt in order to stay in one place. Some live in the silt and mud on the river bed. Others find protection under rocks or amongst the vegetation. The larvae (young form) of some gnats anchor themselves to rocks with sticky threads.

The stonefly spends the first part of its life in water. Stonefly nymphs *(above)* survive in upland rivers by wedging their slender bodies into tiny gaps between stones. They may emerge from the water for short periods, to explore the splash zone for food. They feed on decaying leaf material that is washed down in the current.

△ Caddis flies start life in water. In fast-flowing rivers the larvae *(right)* make cases out of tiny stones to protect them from predators.

River watch

At the edge of slow-moving rivers, you can use a pond net to find small animals. On a small, fast river, stretch a length of fine fishing net across the water. Fix the net to two sticks. Make sure the net is mainly beneath the water. After an hour or so carefully remove the net and tip any creatures into a dish of water. Return the animals to the river as soon as you have studied them.

ALWAYS be careful near water. It is best to have an adult with you.

Freshwater shrimps *(above)* are found in many rivers. When they move, they head upstream, against the current. Crayfish *(left)* are found in rivers running through limestone. They use the lime to build up their shells.

Many kinds of fish live in rivers. Trout and salmon prefer upland rivers, where the cold, rushing water is full of oxygen. Minnows and dace are common further downstream, where the river bed is gravel. Fish such as bream and roach live in still and slow-moving water.

Some fish feed on plants, while others eat insect larvae, worms and even small fish. Fish such as bleak feed on insects that fall into the water from overhanging branches. Some species of fish take both plant and animal food.

The brown trout

Trout eggs are laid on gravel. After five weeks the young alevins hatch *(below)*, and feed on the egg yolk. The alevins develop into young fish, known as fry *(right)* until they are a year old. The adult brown trout *(far right)* may reach 1m in length.

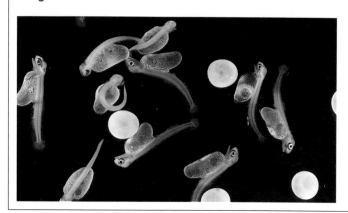

△ The minnow is the smallest member of the carp family. It is usually found in unpolluted upper courses of rivers. Minnows are preyed on by larger fish and the kingfisher. For protection, minnows swim around in large schools.

Bream *(above right)* live in huge shoals. They feed on the bottom, looking for small animals in the mud, especially snails. Large patches of muddy water on the surface are a sign that bream are digging about in the river bed below.

The life of a salmon

Salmon are born in fresh water in rivers, but move downstream to the salt water of the sea when they reach the smolt stage.

Adult salmon return to the river in which they were born, in order to spawn (lay eggs).

eggs

fry (less than one year old)

parr (up to three years old)

The young salmon leave the rivers where they were born and move out to sea to feed. Their feeding grounds are off the coast of Greenland. After two or three years they make their way back to the rivers to spawn.

Iceland

Norway

Greenland

Great Britain

Canada

Atlantic Ocean

adult salmon

smolt (young salmon)

BIRDS OF THE RIVER

Birds of all kinds need water for drinking and bathing, and some feed on water creatures. Upland rivers support only a few birds, but lower down the river the plentiful supply of food attracts many species. Many river birds catch water insects and fish. Others visit rivers to catch insects as they fly over the water on warm summer days.

Rivers also provide ideal nesting areas for some birds. Sand martins burrow into sandy river banks, and reed and sedge warblers build their nests in reed beds. The dipper builds its mossy nest close to water — often on a bridge or under a waterfall.

△ The dipper bobs its head up and down as it stands on a boulder in the river. It goes underwater and runs along the river bed to catch water insects.

▷ The kingfisher hovers or perches by the river searching for fish. It dives to catch its prey and returns immediately to its perch.

△ Wagtails bob their tails up and down. The grey wagtail hunts around pebbles to find insects, and hovers over water to collect midges.

▷ The grey heron is one of the largest birds found by rivers. It feeds by stabbing fish with its long beak.

RIVER MAMMALS

In Britain there are only three native mammals that are found in and around rivers: the water shrew, the water vole and the otter. Other river mammals that are seen by rivers have been introduced from other countries.

Many land mammals visit rivers from time to time. Red deer are excellent swimmers, and can cross large, fast rivers. Foxes sometimes go to rivers, looking for an easy meal. They often take ducks, particularly when the weather is cold and the water partly frozen, so the ducks cannot swim away. The brown rat sometimes lives in holes in the bank.

△ The water vole lives in the river bank. It builds a nest of shredded grass in part of its burrow. Baby voles learn to swim when they are one month old.

▽ The Chinese water deer was introduced to Woburn Park in England in 1900. Some escaped and now live in the wild.

△ American mink were brought into Britain early this century. They were bred on farms to produce fur. Many got out into the wild, where they bred. They stay close to water, and fight each other over their territory.

The otter

Otters live in river banks, in special burrows called holts. The entrance to the holt is usually well hidden by vegetation. Newborn cubs are helpless – they are born blind and have no teeth. They leave the holt for the first time when they are about four months old. Mother otters protect their young fiercely, and may even attack a dog if it threatens their babies.

Otters feed mainly on fish. They take trout and salmon, but they like other food as well. They can even catch moorhens by swimming underneath them, then pulling them under the water.

The otter is a very powerful swimmer. It has a sleek, streamlined body and its tail acts like a ship's rudder. Its toes are webbed, like a duck, so it can paddle very well.

The otter's coat is specially adapted for a wet life. It has two layers which together act like a raincoat and a warm blanket. When the otter dives, the under coat traps air bubbles in the hairs. The bubbles stop water getting to the skin, and keep the animal warm.

Otters keep in contact with other otters by using smell. Their droppings, for example, called spraints, are left in special places – often on ledges or rocks, or under bridges. Spraints have a strong smell and probably indicate an otter's territory.

Some waterfalls were formed thousands of years ago when movements in the Earth's crust made some rocks slip down below other rocks. Others were formed during the last ice age. Large U-shaped valleys were cut in the uplands by the glaciers. Streams often run along these valleys, then drop as waterfalls on to the lower land. Underground, waterfalls occur where the river has worn away the rock in caves.

Waterfalls create very special conditions for wildlife. The crashing water forms a fine spray, which keeps the air moist. Plants and small animals thrive in the damp nooks and crannies worn into the rock.

△ A gentle waterfall can become a torrent after heavy rain. Algae and moss (left) grow on the smooth rocks. No flowering plants can stand up to the force of the water in a waterfall but pink purslane (below) is sometimes seen close by.

At the foot of a waterfall, the rock is worn away to form a hollow area, where the water is quite deep. The force of the falling water causes the water below to swirl round, making a whirlpool. Whirlpools are also formed in the lower course of a river where large rocks jut out and force the water to swirl round. Bends in the river can have the same effect.

Whirlpools in turn affect the river bed. In rivers flowing over clay or sand, the whirlpool gathers up all the coarser gravel beneath it. In rivers with a stony bed, the whirlpool collects together fine silt. So whirlpools provide a habitat that is different from the surrounding river.

△ The pearl mussel is found in fast-flowing rivers. It burrows into the sandy silt at the edge of whirlpools and near boulders. If a grain of sand gets into the mussel shell, a pearl may form round the sand.

▽ This whirlpool is in a fast-flowing chalk river. Under the whirlpool the river bed is covered in silt. The amphibious bistort (inset) sometimes grows in the muddy area at the edge of whirlpools.

River wildlife is more varied if there is an island in the water. Animals are safe from predators and plants are not disturbed by people.

Some islands only last for a few months and are then washed away by heavy rainfall. They form in the summer, when the water level is low, and are made of material deposited by the current. A few plants are able to colonise temporary islands for just one season, which gives them long enough to flower and produce seed. If more plants become settled, silt washed down by the river gradually builds up round them. The island then becomes more permanent.

▽ Colonies of tufted ducks nest together on islands with plenty of plant cover. They dive to find food. They like weeds and grasses, and small freshwater animals.

◁ Mud washed down by the river collects round the base of the flowering rush. After a while, other plants can grow in this mud.

△ The alder can grow with its roots in water. Its timber is very tough, even when wet, and is used to make underwater supports for buildings.

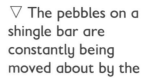

In areas where the rock is very hard, the river cannot wear away the ground quickly. The rock is broken down into shingle (pebbles) on the river bed, instead of fine sand and silt. Shingle sometimes forms islands in rivers, known as shingle bars. They are very unstable and are easily broken down by storm water.

Beneath the shingle there is likely to be fine silty sand. Some plants can grow on shingle bars because they have very deep roots that can reach down to the sand. In upland areas mosses colonise shingle. They trap soil and dead plant particles, in which rushes and sedges can take root.

▽ The pebbles on a shingle bar are constantly being moved about by the water. Few plants can take root on shingle.

△ The oystercatcher is usually seen by the sea, but now nests on shingle bars as well as on the beach. Its nest is just a hollow in the stones, lined with small stones or shells.

▷ The bright flowers of the coltsfoot can be seen on some shingle bars. The flowers appear before the heart-shaped leaves.

Britain has about 3000 miles of canals. They were dug out in the 1700s and 1800s and linked up with most of the big rivers. Canals were used for carrying freight on barges. Today, the canals are used mainly for boating, fishing and other watersports.

Canals provide a water habitat for wildlife that is very different from rivers. The depth of water is about the same from one end of the canal to the other. It is deep in the middle, with shallows at the edges. But the most important difference is that the water only flows very gently. The current is not strong enough to wear away the banks or bed of the canal.

▽ Although boats stop many plants growing in the water of a canal, the banks and towpath edges are a haven for plants and insects.

Dragonflies, and the smaller damselflies like the banded agrion *(above)*, are common by canals. They feed on insects and lay their eggs in the water.

▷ The reed bunting nests in plants beside canals. It feeds on seeds of marsh plants, and insects. In the breeding season the male has a black and white bib and collar.

△ In summer, when the water warms up, algae may cover the water's surface and block out light to the plants below.

▽ Ragged robin thrives in damp places beside ponds, rivers and canals, and in wet meadows and marshes.

△ Yellow iris flowers in spring. In autumn, the seed pods split and drop the seeds into the water, which carries them away.

△ Frogs *(above)*, toads and newts move to ponds, canals and other still or slow-moving water in spring to breed.

Canal wildlife is found in three distinct areas: in the central channel, in the shallows and on the banks. Only a few plants are found in the central channel. The vegetation is cut regularly to keep the way clear for boats. A number of fish, however, do live in this deeper water.

Many water plants flourish in the shallows. The flowers attract many insects, and dragonflies dart across the water in search of insect prey. Along the bank grasses, sedges, brambles and hawthorn grow up to form a shrub zone. Many birds nest among these plants.

Throughout history people have lived and worked beside rivers. People still use rivers today, for transport, to irrigate nearby farmland, to breed fish for food, and so on. Factories that need water are often sited beside rivers. People use rivers for pleasure, too. All these activities affect the wildlife of rivers.

Water from the river can be used to work a water mill. The water is diverted from a nearby river at a weir, and carried along a channel known as a leat. The water flows from the channel into a chute. The chute hangs over the wheel and as the water falls from the chute on to the blades, it pushes the wheel round. The wheel in turn drives machinery inside the mill.

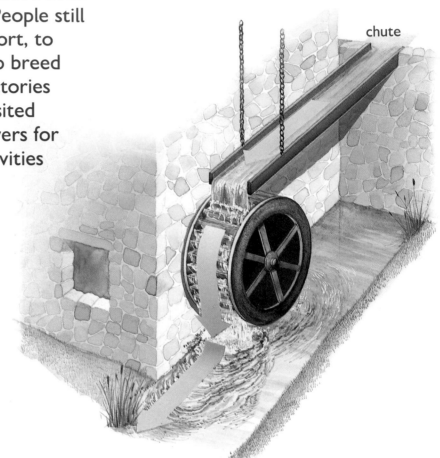

chute

The chute can be extended so that water no longer falls on the wheel, which then stops. The water collects in the mill pond and is taken back to the river along a channel called the tail race.

◁ A traditional way to catch salmon for food was to hang wicker or metal baskets *(far left)* over the river. The leaping salmon *(left)* fell into the baskets when they headed upstream.

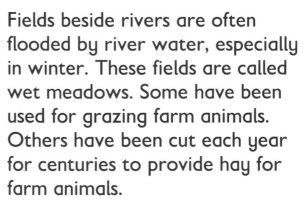

△ Meadowsweet is a heavily scented flower of wet meadows and river banks. The early marsh orchid *(above right)* is fairly common on moist ground.

▷ The snake's head fritillary was once a common flower of wet meadows. It is now very rare.

▽ In summer, a wet meadow is full of colourful wild flowers. In winter, wading birds are attracted by the rich supply of worms and snails in the flooded ground.

Fields beside rivers are often flooded by river water, especially in winter. These fields are called wet meadows. Some have been used for grazing farm animals. Others have been cut each year for centuries to provide hay for farm animals.

These fields are full of wild flowers which benefit from the annual cutting and flooding. The flowers in turn attract many insects. Sadly, many wet meadows have been drained and sprayed with chemicals to provide fields for crops. The plants and insects have mostly disappeared.

THE RIVER MOUTH

The final stretch of a river, where it meets the sea, is known as the river mouth or estuary. Here the fresh water of the river mixes with the salt water of the sea. Silt that is brought down in the river tends to settle in the estuary. It often forms large muddy areas called mudflats.

The estuary can be a difficult place for plants and animals to live. They have to be able to tolerate salt in the water and in the soil. Those that can are often found in large numbers. The amount of salt in the water varies with the state of the tides. At high tide sea water rushes into the river mouth, which makes the river water more salty than at low tide.

Grey mullet *(inset, top)* move into river mouths *(main picture)* to look for worms and algae which they get by sucking up mud.

Flounders *(inset, bottom)* search for worms, shrimps and shellfish which emerge from the mud when the tide comes in.

▽ Sea spurrey grows on mudflats. Its fleshy leaves can hold fresh water.

The mudflats of an estuary are exposed to the air when the tide is out. At low tide in the summer, the mud becomes hot and dry. At low tide in winter mudflats may freeze over. Plants and animals have to be specially adapted to be able to survive in such conditions. Shrimps, worms and shellfish are able to cope with the changing conditions, and they in turn attract many wading birds. The birds use their long bills to probe in the mud to find their food.

△ Shelducks nest in vegetation or in an old rabbit burrow.

▷ The curlew has a long bill that can probe deep into the mud on mudflats.

▽ The Brent goose spends the summer near the Arctic Circle. It visits river estuaries in winter.

A river project

If there is a river near your home or school, look for the river on a map. Make a drawing of the route from its source to the sea. Mark the villages and towns near the river. If you can visit places along the river, make notes about how the river changes along its route. Are there any signs of pollution in your river? Have people changed the river? Try to identify some of the plants and animals that live by the river.

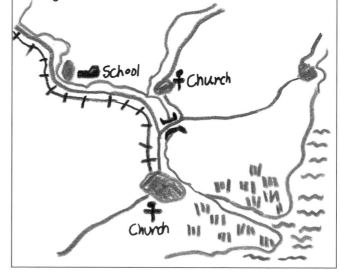

To help you identify river plants, notice which zone they are in. Are they growing on the bank, in the shallows at the river edge, or even floating on the open water? Other habitat clues can help, too. Is the water muddy or clear, slow or fast-moving?

Look down into the water for fish, and signs of underwater burrows that belong to river mammals. Remember to stay very quiet, and always move slowly — most river animals are nervous and will disappear if they hear or see you.

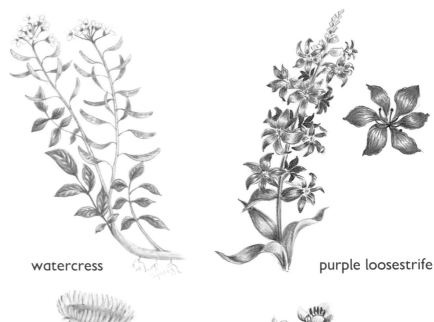

watercress

purple loosestrife

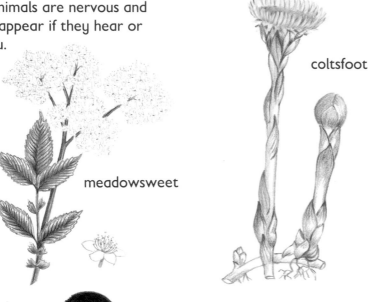

meadowsweet

coltsfoot

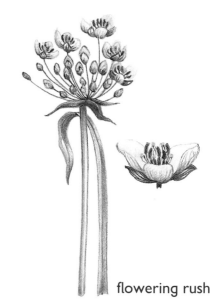

flowering rush

reed bunting

kingfisher

dipper

stonefly nymph

caddis fly larva

freshwater shrimp

minnow

brown trout

bream

white willow

alder

Spot the plants and insects

Now that you have read about rivers, test your knowledge and see if you can identify the plants and animals that have appeared at the top of some of the pages in this book. You will find the answers to the quiz on the next page.

Answers to quiz: page 1 alder, p2 watercress, p3 bream, p5 caddis fly larva, p7 willow, p9 minnow, p11 flowering rush, p13 stonefly nymph, p15 kingfisher, p16 meadowsweet, p19 freshwater shrimp, p21 reed bunting, p23 purple loosestrife, p25 brown trout, p27 dipper, p29 coltsfoot.